D0763488

Here is one example, an excerpt from a recent article in the respected Silicon Valley newspaper, The Mercury News.

"It's my angry belief that most self-help and education book writers get paid by the word. Actually, it's worse than that. Most get paid by the character. This means lots of pointlessly long words, ridiculously complex sentences and page after page after page—you get the idea—of drivel. Three and four hundred page books that could have been done better in 50 pages.

No wonder college students sleep until noon. It isn't the sex, drugs, and rock and roll. No way! They have to read this garbage every day! Personally, I'd rather read the phone book.

Not so with 'The Skinny On' series. These books kick rears and take names. Using entertaining writing, stick figure drawings and a comic book style layout, they use simple stories to quickly convey valuable information.

Each book is like a university class without the fuddy-duddy professor. YIPPEE! Each slender, practical, engaging book can be read in an hour or so. And each gives the kind of advice you might get from a kindly, extremely knowledgeable grandfather.

Highly recommended. Author Jim Randel has created one of the best, most interesting series I've seen in a very long time."

National Library of Australia Cataloguing-in-Publication entry
Creator: Randel, Jim, author.

Title: The skinny on time management : how to maximize your 24-hour gift / Jim Randel.

ISBN: 9781925265460 (paperback)

Subjects: Time management.

Dewey Number: 650.11

Illustration/Design: Lindy Nass
Rebecca Kunzmann

For information address Rand Media Co, 265 Post Road West, Westport, CT, 06880 or call (203) 226-8727.

For information about Skinny books, contact RAND Media Co, 265 Post Road West, Westport, Connecticut 06880, or call 203-226-8727. Ask for Jeannette Zolan or Roberta Bjornson.

Or, visit our website at www.randmediaco.com

Published by:
Wilkinson Publishing Pty Ltd
ACN O06 042 173
Level 4, 2 Collins Street
Melbourne, Vic 3000
Ph: O3 9654 5446
www.wilkinsonpublishing.com.au

Printed in Australia

WP

the skinny on™
time management
how to maximize
your 24-hour gift

Jim Randel

the skinny on™

Welcome to a new series of publications titled **The Skinny On™,** a progression of drawings, dialogue and text intended to convey information in a concise and entertaining fashion.

In our time-starved and information-overloaded culture, most of us have far too little time to read. As a result, our understanding of important subjects often tends to float on the surface—without the insights of writings from thinkers and teachers who have spent years studying these subjects.

Our series is intended to address this situation. Our team of readers and researchers has done a ton of homework preparing our books for you. We read everything we could find on the topic at hand and spoke with the experts. Then we mixed in our own experiences and distilled what we have learned into this "skinny" book for your benefit.

Our goal is to do the reading for you, identify what is important, distill the key points, and present them in a book that is both instructive and enjoyable to read.

Although minimalist in design, we do take our message very seriously. Please do not confuse format with content. The time you invest reading this book will be paid back to you many, many times over.

INTRODUCTION

"Simplicity is the ultimate sophistication." **Steve Jobs**

OK, so what's with the stick people?

It's my premise that many non-fiction writers are out of control. These authors figure it's better to use 20 words when one will do. They write 250 page books (or e-books) and hope that people will read them. This is, in my view, a disrespect and misunderstanding of the 21st century, non-fiction reader.

Readers today have limited time, short attention spans, the internet for information, and no patience for excess. For these reasons, it is incumbent on anyone who wants to convey substantive content to distill it to its most salient points.

Add to this that anyone can "publish" a book today. I count about 100 e-books published in 2015 on time management subjects. Does anyone think each of these books has unique content? NO, NO… All of these books repeat the same 40 - 50 points that someone should understand about time management.

My goal is to identify these 40 - 50 points and in a minimalist style and easy-to-read format, convey them to the readers of my books. I also add in a thin story line, a dash of sophomoric humor, and a goofy moderator. My objective is to give people a decent one-hour read - outlining the key points of time management - and then provide a bibliography for those who want to do a deep dive into the subject.

This approach is not the result of my personal point of view. Many studies have shown that people have a better understanding of a subject when explanations are condensed. One study tested two groups of readers - one having read a 20-page explanation of a subject, and the other having read a 2-page summary. No surprise - the summary readers had higher comprehension.

In addition, recent studies have shown that many more people than originally thought are VISUAL learners. My approach is much more successful in transmitting information to a visual learner than a 200 page, single spaced book.

And so, the Skinny On series. I am sure some people (especially the traditionalists) will hate what I do. That is OK with me. I subscribe to the words of Nobel Prize winning playwright, Maurice Maeterlinck:

"At every crossroads on the path that leads to the future, tradition has placed 10,000 men to guard the past."

"Time is the quality of nature that keeps events from happening all at once. Lately it doesn't seem to be working so well."

Anonymous

Hi, I'm Jim Randel, the founder of **The Skinny On** book series. I will be your guide for the next hour.

Welcome to my home. I've converted my garage into a classroom, and I'd like to use it today to teach you about time management.

CLICK!

2

Notice the bikes. They are there for a reason. One, I like to bike. Two, I want you to understand that although time management is a critical factor in one's success, that does not mean good time managers spend their lives darting from one activity to the other. There are instances when I ride my bike to places just because I enjoy a slow bike ride.

3

And before we take off darting into a study of time management, let's not forget that faster is not always better. Sometimes PATIENCE is required. Many of us tend to suffer from the need to DO, DO, DO...that can be a negative at times. Remember that "a watched pot never boils."

4

A WATCHED POT NEVER BOILS

Come on, come on...

5

"*Patience is bitter, but its fruit is sweet.*"

Jean-Jacques Rousseau
(famous French philosopher)

OK, enough with the talk about patience, I am anxious to get started. Today we are going to discuss how to make the best use of your time in order to optimize the probability that you will achieve your goals. I won't suggest you give up biking or walking or gazing at the stars. I just want you to understand the importance of using time effectively…as and when you desire.

Time is a quickly moving asset. You only have so much of it. What you do with the time you have will be critical to your future.

In many ways, time is your most valuable commodity—waste it at your risk.

Everyone gets 168 hours a week or 720 hours per month.

Every hour counts.

That's why I have this hour glass. I want you to be able to finish my course in just 60 minutes. I don't want to waste one minute of your time.

WHAT IS TIME MANAGEMENT?

TIME MANAGEMENT IS THE APPLICATION OF STRATEGIES AND TECHNIQUES THAT HELP YOU USE YOUR TIME AS EFFECTIVELY AS POSSIBLE.

1. IN THE FIRST HALF OF OUR CLASS, WE WILL REVIEW **HOW YOU ARE PRESENTLY SPENDING YOUR TIME**.

Are you aware of where the hours are going? Are you spending time in a way to move you closer to your goals? Are you making good choices?

2. IN THE SECOND HALF OF OUR CLASS, WE WILL ANALYZE WHETHER YOU ARE **USING YOUR HOURS TO MAXIMUM EFFECTIVENESS**.

The goal here is to make sure that you are utilizing your hours as powerfully as possible.

PART I

A REVIEW OF HOW YOU
ARE SPENDING YOUR TIME

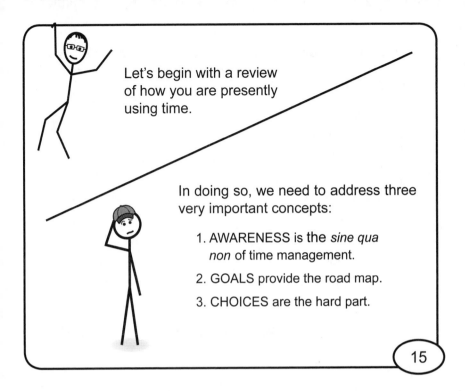

Let's begin with a review of how you are presently using time.

In doing so, we need to address three very important concepts:

1. AWARENESS is the *sine qua non* of time management.
2. GOALS provide the road map.
3. CHOICES are the hard part.

AWARENESS

You cannot be an effective time manager unless you are attuned to the passage of time. I wear a runner's watch 24 hours a day because I like to see the seconds flying by—it helps remind me of how quickly time passes!

As a first exercise, I would like you to write down your best guess as to how you spent the last 72 hours. Make general categories and assign hours to each category.

This does not have to be super precise. It's just meant to start you thinking.

Here is a chart you can use. Or create your own.

Sleeping:	_____ hours
Eating:	_____ hours
Study/Reading:	_____ hours
Watching TV:	_____ hours
Online:	_____ hours
Phone/Texting:	_____ hours
Exercise:	_____ hours
Class or work time:	_____ hours
Recreation:	_____ hours
Miscellaneous:	_____ hours
TOTAL:	**72 hours**

You just took the first step to creating a time journal - allocating the hours of your day into different activities. In this way, you can analyze whether you are using your time in a manner that is most conducive to achieving your goals.

In the past I have kept a time journal. Each day for one week, at the end of the day, I would write down how I spend the preceding 24 hours.

#1 Awareness is the
Sine Qua Non

HERE IS WHAT ONE DAY IN MY TIME JOURNAL LOOKS LIKE:

Time Management Evaluation

TIME	MONDAY	TUESDAY	WEDNESDAY
Midnight			
12:30			
1:00am			
1:30	Sleep		
2:00am			
2:30			
3:00am			
3:30			
4:00am			
4:30			
5:00am			
5:30	Write		
6:00am			
6:30			
7:00am			
7:30			
8:00am	Breakfast-		
8:30	Shower		
9:00am	Dress		
9:30			
10:00am			
10:30			
11:00am	Research		
11:30			
NOON			
12:30			
1:00pm	Lunch		
1:30			
2:00pm			
2:30			
3:00pm	Phone - Email		
3:30			
4:00pm			
4:30	Exercise		
5:00pm			
5:30			
6:00pm	Dinner		
6:30			
7:00pm			
7:30	Baseball game		
8:00pm	on TV.		
8:30			
9:00pm	Online		
9:30			
10:00pm	Read		
10:30			
11:00pm			

Then at the end of the week, I totaled how much time I spent in various general categories.

Sleeping:	49 hours
Eating:	15 hours
Study/Reading (research):	10 hours
Watching TV (sports):	15 hours
Online (e-mails):	7 hours
Phone/texting:	5 hours
Exercise:	10 hours
Class or Work Time (writing):	40 hours
Recreation (meditation, biking):	7 hours
Miscellaneous:	10 hours
TOTAL:	168 hours

20

And you know what? I surprised myself by how much time I was spending watching sports—about 15 hours of every week. I decided this was too much if I was going to keep to my schedule of writing 6 books a year.

I realized that if I cut back my TV time to 7.5 hours per week, I would have about 30 additional hours every month in which to write, or 360 hours per year. In that time I could write one or two more books.

Sleeping:	49 hours
Eating:	15 hours
Study/Reading (research):	10 hours
Watching TV (sports):	15 hours
Online (e-mails):	7 hours
Phone/texting:	5 hours
Exercise:	10 hours
Class or Work Time (writing):	40 hours
Recreation (meditation, biking):	7 hours
Miscellaneous:	10 hours
TOTAL:	168 hours

21

Does it seem odd to you that I did not know how much time I was spending watching sports? In one way, I did know of course. It's just that by forcing myself to total up the hours—against the 168 hours I had in the week—I could not ignore the fact that I was spending almost 13% of my waking hours watching sports.

Certain activities are seductive of course. We do them with good intentions of limiting ourselves to a specific amount of time UNTIL time seems to slip. It flies by. We lose track of time and spend more than we had planned.

22

I am sure that you have heard of Albert Einstein. He is famous for many things including the theory of relativity, E = MC squared, which basically means… well, actually I have no idea what it means. But, no matter, I have my own theory of relativity.

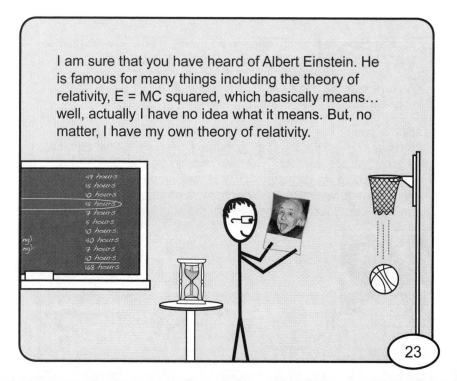

23

My theory of relativity says that how we experience time depends upon what we are doing. I have indicated that I lose track of time when I am watching sports on TV. Minutes pass quickly. But, when I come home at the end of a day, starving, and throw something into the microwave, a five-minute wait seems like forever.

My point here is that you need to be aware of how you experience time. What are you doing when time flies? When it drags?

An awareness of how you experience time can tell you a lot about yourself.

How a person experiences time is a window into his or her passions. The objective is to consume time in a way that creates a good balance between your passions, goals, and recreations. I love watching sports but too much of that interferes with my need and desire to write. On the other hand, if all I do is write, then it becomes drudgery for me - impacting the quality of my work.

Self-awareness is critical for three reasons:

1. By increasing awareness as to how you spend time, you may discover areas where adjustments are appropriate, such as my decision to reduce the time I was watching sports.

2. By gaining a better understanding of how you spend time, you may find opportunities to pick up productive time. Trying to be helpful, I recently mentioned to my wife that her average daily shower was 15 minutes, and that if she could get it down to ten minutes, she could pick up an additional 2.5 hours of productive time every month. She told me that if I ever brought that up again, she would knock me silly.

14:29,
14:30,
14:31...

3. Just by focusing on time, by keeping a journal, you start to think of time as a fleeting asset. Making a journal sensitizes you as to how you are spending your depreciating asset—the hours of your life.

OK, now that you understand the importance of awareness, do you want to take a guess at the meaning of the Latin expression *sine qua non*?

The translation of *sine qua non* is **without which, nothing.**

It means that if you do not have an awareness of how you are spending time, you have no ability to manage your time effectively. There is no point fooling yourself.

That is why self-awareness is the first step!

GOALS

OK, time is flying. We now need to discuss my second concept—by defining goals, we begin to highlight the route we need to take.

"Goals are the fuel in the furnace of achievement."

Anonymous

You can't decide where you should allocate your time unless and until you determine exactly where it is you want to go. That is why I call goal setting the road map.

Goal setting is about deciding today where you want to be, and what you want to be doing, say in 6 months…or one year…or five years.

There is no accepted standard as to what is a short-term goal and what is a longer-term goal. Just so we have something to work with, let's call any goal that can be achieved within one year a short-term goal and all other goals long-term.

For purposes of our discussion, let's also distinguish a goal from a task. When I use the word "task," I am speaking to a chore or job or errand that must be accomplished in the very near term.

On your <u>To Do List</u> you put <u>Tasks</u>;
On your <u>Mission Statement</u> you put <u>Goals</u>.

One of my objectives with this book is to get you thinking... about your goals, your dreams, your best-case scenario.

You

What are your goals? What do you hope to accomplish in the short term? What do you want your life to look like in the long term?

"How do you plan on getting from where you are to where you want to be? What are the steps from here to there?

Who knew he'd be asking such difficult questions in a course on time management? I need some time to reflect.

I don't mean to be intrusive but if you don't know where you want your life to be in the near and far term, then you don't know what steps you must take, and what kind of time you need to allocate to each step.

Once you have identified your goals, you can better identify the steps you need to take, and the time commitments you need to make.

The following is an example of a goals-steps-time analysis i did recently with my daughter, now beginning her third year of college.

What is important is that you see the process of connecting goals and time.

My daughter's goal was to obtain a 3.5 GPA in the fall semester of her junior year. Note that the statement of her goal met four important criteria:

(i) it was specific (3.5 GPA),

(ii) it had a time frame (fall semester),

(iii) it was realistic (she knew she was capable), and

(iv) it was important to the goal-setter (this was my daughter's idea).

My daughter will be taking 12 credits in the fall. That means 12 hours of class time per week. She decided that she would need to spend 2.5 hours of time outside class for every hour in class if she was going to achieve a 3.5 GPA. The 2.5 hours included class assignments, preparation, reading, and study time for tests and quizzes. So that required another 30 hours per week (12 x 2.5).

So, total school time = 42 hours (class and outside class).

Then my daughter listed all her other activities during the week and the hours she needed for each.

UH OH.

12 hours class time
30 hours outside class time
56 hours sleeping
20 hours shower, dress, eat, back and forth to class
20 hours practice – cross country team
15 hours with friends
8 hours on phone or online
12 hours miscellaneous chores and obligations

TOTAL : 173 hours

And this is when she realized her problem. She needs 173 hours a week to fit in everything she wants to do! Unfortunately, in the game of life, we only get 168 hours a week.

37

This analysis showed my daughter that if she really wanted to achieve a 3.5 GPA, she was going to have to make some changes in how she spends her time. Perhaps she will have to sleep less. Or spend less time eating and dressing for school. Or cut back on the hours she spends with friends.

#2 Goals provide the road map

38

I am using this example to make a point. Whatever your goal, there will be action steps you need to take to achieve it. Those steps will take time. Do you have the time? Are you prepared to take time from other activities in order to find the time you need?

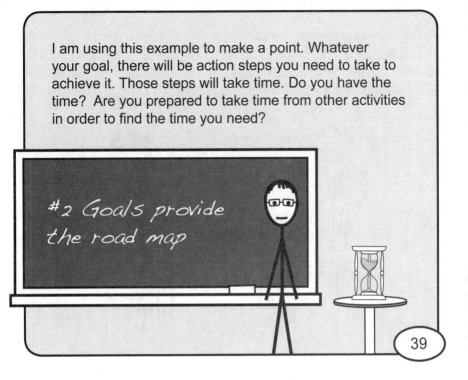

#2 Goals provide the road map

But what if I don't know all the steps I need to take to achieve my goals? What if I don't know the time I need for the steps I do know?

YOU

Excellent question...I am happy to see that you are paying such careful attention and that you are thinking about what I am saying.

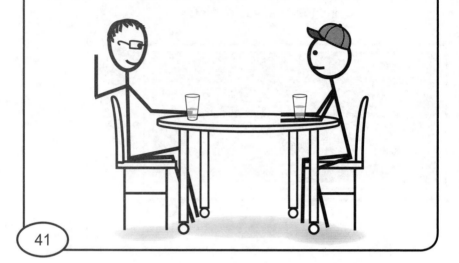

41

There may be several steps between where you are and where you want to be that are either unknown or unclear to you. That's fine. Just by beginning to contemplate the passage from here to there, three important things start to happen:

42

First, just by thinking about steps and time, you engage your analytical and creative juices. You move the ball forward in understanding what you have to do to get where you want to be.

Second, whether you realize it or not, you are starting to plan. You are starting to actually visualize the achievement of your goals. Visualization increases desire, which increases intensity.

Third, you are testing your resolve. By identifying specific steps and time requirements, you double check your intensity for certain goals. There may be situations, in fact, when you make a conscious decision to put off the pursuit of one of your goals because you conclude you don't have the desire to do what is required to go from here to there.

All I am trying to do at this point in our session is to help you conceptualize a goals-steps-time analysis.

This is not an exact science. I am just suggesting you begin the process of integrating goal-setting and time management.

LET'S RECAP:

1. BY BECOMING MORE **AWARE** OF HOW YOU ARE USING TIME, YOU IDENTIFY AREAS WHERE YOU MAY WANT TO MAKE CHANGES.

2. BY DEFINING YOUR **GOALS**, YOU BEGIN TO ESTABLISH A ROAD MAP FROM WHERE YOU ARE TO WHERE YOU WANT TO BE.

CHOICES

All of this leads to the third major concept with respect to your use…or abuse…of time. Dreams don't come easily, choices need to be made.

#3 Choices are the hard part

Once you become aware of how you use your time and have a basic road map to your goals, the nuts and bolts of the analysis are complete. Now, however, comes the hard part.

Now you need to do a gut check. You need to find a balance between living for the moment—doing exactly what you want to do right now, and living for the future—putting yourself in a position to lead the life you want at some point down the road.

I need to get closer to you right now. I need to tell you something really important about life: **LIFE IS NOT FAIR**.

I am not going to stand here and tell you that if you work very hard you can be anything you want. Life just does not work that way. There are factors and events beyond your control that will impact how your life plays out.

But what I can tell you is this: By making the right choices, by putting yourself in a position to succeed, you maximize the chances you will achieve whatever it is that you want.

Time management is in large part about choices. Now that you have a heightened sense of time and have set some goals, you need to confront competing pressures. Calls from friends. The desire to sleep late. Commitments and obligations. The seduction of the internet. Anything that pulls you from what you need to do to achieve your goals.

"Successful people do not enjoy doing the things that others do not. Successful people simply do them nevertheless."

The Study of Success, E.N. Gray

At this point in the book I want to introduce you to a very entertaining lecture about time management given by Randy Pausch, formerly Professor of Computer Sciences at Carnegie Mellon.

Professor Pausch's story is poignant.

At age 40, Professor Pausch, father of three young children, learned that he had pancreatic cancer and was dying. He actually lived for 18 months after his diagnosis and during that period he wrote a best-selling book (*The Last Lecture*). He also gave a guest lecture on **time management** at the University of Virginia.

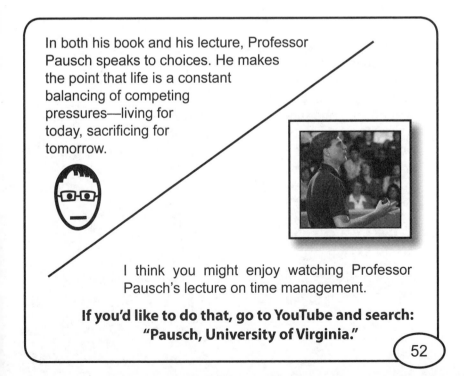

In both his book and his lecture, Professor Pausch speaks to choices. He makes the point that life is a constant balancing of competing pressures—living for today, sacrificing for tomorrow.

I think you might enjoy watching Professor Pausch's lecture on time management.

If you'd like to do that, go to YouTube and search: "Pausch, University of Virginia."

OK, enough talking for the moment...my cell phone is vibrating which means it's time for me to take a 20 minute break to meditate. I find that if I meditate for just 20 minutes every day, I increase my energy, my serenity, and my productivity.

#3 Choices are the hard part

I realize that it can at times be hard to find 20 minutes to meditate every day. But, please try.

And, as an older person, let me tell you something important: One reason to work hard when you are young is so that you can do what you want, and when you want, as your life moves on.

While I am meditating you might want to take a few minutes to try a fun online self-assessment test which claims to measure what kind of time manager you are. Here's the link:

www.literacynet.org/icans/chapter03/timemgmt.html

When I meditate I put on a playlist of soft music timed to exactly twenty minutes so that when the music stops, I know to stop meditating. If I did not do that, I might be lost in mindlessness for hours.

By the way, I don't usually wear a blindfold when I meditate. I just thought it would be a cute visual metaphor for what it's like going through life without an awareness of how you spend your time.

Wow…do I feel refreshed!

And while I was meditating a thought popped into my head. That happens often…which is one reason to meditate. By quieting the noise, you clear space in your mind for new ideas and thoughts.

The thought is this: **I don't want you to be frantic about not knowing exactly what you want to do with your life.**

For most people goal setting is about identifying general directions. Life often takes twists and turns that no one can predict. Still, by constantly reflecting on your goals and readjusting at times, you increase the probability that your life will proceed on your agenda—and not someone else's or, simply by fate.

#3 Choices are the hard part

PART II

USING THE HOURS YOU HAVE
TO MAXIMUM EFFECTIVENESS

We've now come to the midpoint of our class. It's now time to turn to a review of how effective you are with the time you have.

From here on, we are going to talk about strategies and techniques for using what time you do have as powerfully as possible.

I am going to switch to my laptop now and use a screen. I get tired of writing on the blackboard. Blackboards are so yesterday.

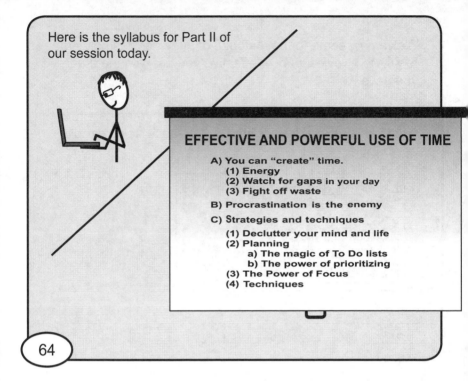

EFFECTIVE AND POWERFUL USE OF TIME

A) You can "create" time.
    (1) Energy
    (2) Watch for gaps in your day
    (3) Fight off waste

B) Procrastination is the enemy

C) Strategies and techniques
    (1) Declutter your mind and life
    (2) Planning
        a) The magic of To Do lists
        b) The power of prioritizing
    (3) The Power of Focus
    (4) Techniques

Here is the syllabus for Part II of our session today.

64

In the second half of our class, we are going to learn the strategies and techniques really successful people employ to get the most out of every hour.

The first topic I want to discuss is how we can create more time in our lives.

65

As you can see, I've typed on the screen, "Time is Finite." But, wait, didn't I just say that there are ways to create time? How can that be if time is finite? Am I losing my marbles?

Well, perhaps, but here is my point: Whereas time is finite, there are ways to turn unproductive time into productive time. That's the same as finding more hours in the day ... of "creating" time for yourself.

TIME IS FINITE

Let me give you an example.

That's what I look like early in the morning when the alarm goes off. Half asleep—half awake. No one enjoys lazing in bed more than I do.

But you know what? By training myself to jump out of bed **as soon as** the alarm goes off instead of laying in bed like I used to, I gain ten minutes a day times 365, or about 60 extra hours of time over the course of a year. That's almost 3 extra days a year of productive time!

OK, OK…I hear you. You don't care about gaining 3 extra days a year. You would rather have ten additional minutes in bed every morning.

I understand! Leisure and rest are critical to a happy life. I am just trying to make the point that there are ways to CREATE time you can use as you see fit.

I recently read a good book about BALANCE - finding a comfortable spot between what the author calls your fast world (high tech, digital devices) and your slow world (contemplation and reflection).

Mindful Tech: How to Bring Balance to Our Digital Lives,

David M. Levy (Yale University Press, 2016)

No easy answer—just that you need to be very aware of how your intense and reactive digital life steals time from your meditative and introspective life.

OK, let's go to the next slide. HEY! How did that get in here? My wife must be playing a joke on me. Here, let me get rid of that...

Please forgive my wife's little joke. Stick people are not very modest. I don't even know if I'm naked right now. Stick people have debated that subject for years.

70

71

MATCHING TIME AND ENERGY

Effective time management is not just about finding additional hours in the day. Impactful time management is also about matching up your available time with your available energy.

To make my point, I would like to borrow a phrase from a famous 20th century American writer named Gertrude Stein.

Ms. Stein penned the well-known phrase "a rose is a rose is a rose." Her point was that whatever name you choose to give something, you don't change the essence of what it is. Another way of saying the same thing is that "if it walks like a duck, swims like a duck, and quacks like a duck, it must be a duck."

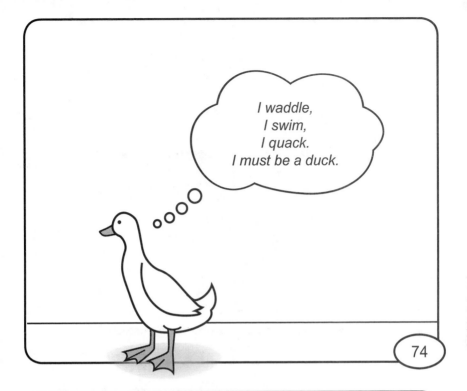

What do Gertrude Stein and ducks have to do with time management? Well, they are just set-up's for another point we need to discuss: **in your pursuit of effective time management, not all hours are alike**.

In order to make each of your hours as effective as possible, you should attempt to perform your hardest tasks during those hours when you are the most alert…when you have the most energy. I happen to be an early bird. I am really flying (excuse the metaphor) at 4 AM and I write well at that hour. But, check back with me at about 10 PM and I can barely talk, let alone write.

AN HOUR IS NOT AN HOUR IS NOT AN HOUR

My wife on the other hand is a night owl. She hates the early morning. She gets her best work done late at night.

To be most effective, you need to attack your challenges when you have maximum energy.

This is me at 10 PM.

You can also take steps to optimize your energy level.

No magic there…exercise daily, eat healthy, get lots of fluids, moderate your intake of caffeine and alcohol.

With a healthy lifestyle you can boost your productivity by turning unproductive hours into productive hours as you increase your energy levels.

98, 99, 100 …

Not bad for an old guy, huh? 100 push-ups at age 60. My goal is actually to do 60 push-ups at age 100! First goal: live to 100.

When do you have your most energy? Use the time when you have the most energy to tackle your ugliest, most difficult chores. In this way you are most likely to finish them in the shortest possible time. That is effective time management.

GOAL:
AGE: 100
PUSH-UPS 60

Some experts even suggest that the key to productivity is to focus not on time, but on energy. For an excellent book on the time and energy analysis, you might want to pick up:

The Power of Full Engagement: Managing Energy, Not Time, is the Key to High Performance and Personal Renewal

Jim Loehr and Tony Schwartz (Free Press, 2003)

I feel like I need to speak to you about getting enough sleep.

Most experts suggest a minimum of 7 hours of sleep in a 24-hour cycle. Yet many of us try to "beat the system" by cutting back on our sleep. BAD IDEA. Sleep is important for good health, for energy, for clear thinking.

"Cognitive performance deteriorates when sleep is inadequate: We have less capacity to remember, to learn or to be creative...And those consequences aren't reserved for just extreme sleep loss: Studies show that two weeks of sleeping only six hours a night can have the same impact as one or two nights of total sleep deprivation."

Get Some Sleep and Wake Up the GDP,

The New York Times (Feb, 2014)

OK. Now let's talk about another area where you can "create" time - gaps in your day. Downtimes. Short periods when you are between A and B with nothing specific to do.

Right after our session today I have to go to the dentist. You may not know this but stick people have a very low pain threshold, and so I really hate the dentist.

Since my dentist knows I am a bit of a cry-baby, he gives me a lot of novocaine and waits ten minutes before working on me. During that ten minutes I get a lot of work done on my cell phone.

Utilizing downtime while in the dentist's chair is only one example of what I am talking about. We all have gaps in our day. By always having something to do during these gaps, we "create" time by turning unproductive minutes into productive ones.

Please take a few moments to think about gaps in your typical week. Times when are you shuffling your feet instead of doing something productive. Think of ways to use this time more effectively.

GAPS

HOW TO USE THE GAP MORE EFFECTIVELY

1. _____   1. _____

2. _____   2. _____

3. _____   3. _____

86

Good time managers always know how to find time for the things they need to get done.

My wife is a college professor and she teaches her students that finding time is like filling a pickle jar. HUH? Yes, I know. I said the same thing when she first said that to me.

87

Nope! Now I am pouring in a lot of small pebbles that fit between the golf balls. Full?

Nope! Now I am putting in sand which falls between the golf balls and pebbles. Has to be full now!

IF YOU WANT HELP WITH GETTING A PROJECT DONE, ASK THE BUSIEST PERSON YOU KNOW.

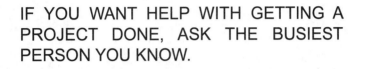

"Waste not, want not."

Benjamin Franklin

Effective time management is about a minimum of waste. Did you ever notice how great athletes are very fluid? There is little wasted motion or energy.

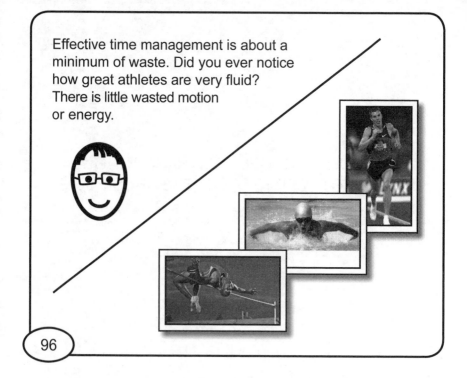

Similarly, great time managers become excellent at minimizing waste. They learn to build efficiency into their lives. Here are three examples of how they do that:

1. Make decisions quickly—tremendous waste comes out of indecision. As soon as you have the facts you need to make a decision, do so.

2. Speed reading—I will be speaking more about this later, but here is the key—do not try to read every word of whatever it is you are reading **(except Skinny books of course)**. Too many writers use 10 words to communicate when 5 would do. Learn to read just the five.

3. Improve memorization skills. People with good memories operate at a higher level of efficiency than others.

Let's spend a minute or two on memorization skills.

IMPROVING YOUR MEMORY

1. Stretch your mind. I do a crossword puzzle almost every day. I find that doing so forces me to push myself mentally, to see words and phrases in different ways. To work at my skills of recollection. I am convinced this practice helps my memory. There are tons of puzzles and games you can do. Some people believe video games improve memory.

"Scientists are increasingly examining the potential benefits of video games. Their studies are revealing that a wide variety of games can boost mental function, improving everything from vision to memory."

Boston Globe, **Emily Anthes, October 2009**

2. Spread out your intake of food and drink. When you overload yourself with food and/or drink, your sugar level spikes ... and then shortly thereafter drops dramatically. This causes an energy loss which reduces your mental recall. By taking in less food/drink in any one sitting, you decrease the likelihood of this happening.

3. Exercise. The usual biggie. Exercise increases blood flow to the brain. Studies have shown that exercise reduces the prospect of Alzheimer's. Exercise also has a calming effect which reduces stress and settles the mind.

4. Antioxidants. Foods containing antioxidants such as berries, broccoli, and spinach, appear to improve mental function. Ditto for Omega-3 fatty acids (think fish). We can't say for sure that these food groups will help your memory, but they will make you healthier, so nothing lost!

5. Learn memory skills. I am not great with names so I develop little games to help me recall a person's name. For example, when I meet a person for the first time, I immediately try to picture him or her with a Post-It note on his/her forehead. On this note is his/her name. For some reason, seeing the name in writing helps me.

"Nice to meet you, YOU."

6. Perform associations or rhymes. The combination on my bike lock is 42-32-10. I had trouble remembering it until I made up a goofy statement for myself:

*"Hey, Jim, you don't look **42**.*
*You don't even look **32**. You're a **10**!"*

OK, silly, I admit but somehow it helps me remember!

7. Get enough sleep. There is an expression that "fatigue makes cowards of us all." The point is that we are never at our best when running on empty. That goes for mental productivity as well.

8. Concentrate. I am convinced that one reason people forget things is that they do not concentrate when they first hear a fact, meet a person ... whatever. When you are about to read something that is important to remember, take note and focus. Just that act will improve your powers of recall.

9. Convert important facts into a format that assists your recall. I am always working at improving my vocabulary which is, in part, about memory—i.e., the ability to pull up words to use as and when you want them. One way I do that is by writing down words and definitions that are new to me. I then write down the word in a sentence. The act of writing helps me.

10. Don't stress about your memory skills. Sometimes memory problems come because we stress that we don't have a good memory. It is like a self-fulfilling prophecy: we think we don't have a good memory, so we stress and, **as a result**, we don't have a good memory. You have a better memory than you think. It's just that you can probably make it a little better.

OK, enough about memory skills. Now I must have been making some larger point...I don't remember ...

Just goofing! Of course I remember my point: By utilizing gaps in your day and by cutting down on wasted motion—like indecision, overly slow reading and poor memory—you can make yourself incredibly more efficient.

100

NOW ON TO A REALLY, REALLY BIG TOPIC

101

Lots of people have good intentions. They tell you what they are going to do "someday." But "someday" never turns into "today." These people procrastinate their lives away.

"When all is said and done, more is said than done."

Anonymous

Procrastination is the result of a very powerful law of physics known as INERTIA.

Inertia states that a body at rest will remain at rest until acted on by some outside force. In other words, things—including people—tend to stay put. In order to achieve forward motion, people need to push themselves. Inertia tends to keep us all in place.

INERTIA

I used to be a procrastinator. I always had good reasons why not to start on a project or task. Sometimes the magnitude of the project intimidated me. Sometimes I did not know how to start. And sometimes I was just being lazy. In fact, I used to subscribe to Mark Twain's advice:

"Never put off for tomorrow what you can put off until the day after tomorrow."

But then one day it hit me. I was only hurting myself. No one really cared how my life played out...except me. I realized that if I wanted to make something with my life, I needed to stop making excuses.

Little by little, I forced myself to fight back against inertia. I reached a point in my life when an impulse to be lazy was overwhelmed by a fear of looking back with regret on missed opportunities.

STRATEGIES FOR DEFEATING PROCRASTINATION:

1. Keep a piece of paper or index card in your pocket with your goals written in bold ink. People who are adept at warding off procrastination are able to connect the result of their action (or inaction) with the achievement of their goals (or lack thereof). By keeping reminders of your goals handy, you are less likely to delay steps that can bring you closer to your personal dreamscape.

2. Break big projects up into manageable pieces. Most of us are overwhelmed when contemplating a huge project. We look at the height of the mountain in front of us and we think, *"What's the use?"* By dividing that project up into smaller pieces, or by just taking a step forward (even if a small step), the height of the mountain becomes a bit smaller and less intimidating.

3. Train your mind (awareness) to recognize the first signs of laziness or procrastination. We can all feel ourselves getting tired or lazy. We know we should do something but just don't feel like it. When you first begin to experience that feeling, that is the precise time to jump right up and get going. This is a procrastination-busting reflex that can be developed and strengthened.

4. Always carry a means of taking notes. Your cell phone (or good old-fashioned pad and paper) can be used to memorialize thoughts or ideas. At times you may not have an opportunity to start a project but you can at least make an outline, or a To Do List, or just scribble down some ideas. Putting those thoughts in writing will help propel you into action the next chance you have to get started.

By the way, there is some good news about inertia: It is actually **two** forces of nature. One that tends to keep immobile objects in place **AND** another that keeps moving objects moving. This means that once you fight off the impulse to stay put, to do nothing, and start moving forward, you will be **the beneficiary** of inertia. It's like having the wind at your back.

INERTIA CAN ALSO
BE YOUR FRIEND

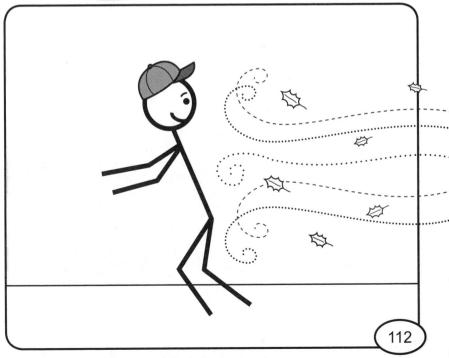

The point is that you can beat procrastination. After all, procrastination is all in your mind. While there are challenges you will face in life that are not within your control, fighting off procrastination is not one of those.

People who develop the mental strength and fortitude to beat back the impulses to procrastinate are well on their way to achieve their dreams.

PROCRASTINATION IS A DREAM KILLER

113

Time management and mental fortitude go hand in hand.

Those who develop mental strength are more likely to:

(i) keep on schedule/plan;

(ii) make good choices;

(iii) maintain focus; and

(iv) defeat procrastination.

MENTAL FORTITUDE IS A SKILL THAT CAN BE DEVELOPED

114

I have studied mental fortitude for 25 years. I do not believe people are either born with it...or not. Rather, I believe it is a skill that can be developed like any other.

Here are the three points to understand in order to begin developing strong mental fortitude:

1. **You are not your mind**. Rather, you are the higher being hearing your thoughts. As a result, you have dominion over negative thoughts in your head—thoughts, for example, of procrastination or laziness.

Eckhart Tolle makes this point in *The Power of Now*:

"The single most important step you can take is to learn to dis-identify from your mind. At some point you will smile at the thoughts in your mind, as if they are antics of a small child."

2. **Thoughts are things just like a tangible object.** Napoleon Hill makes this point in his excellent book, **Think & Grow Rich**, written in 1936. When you conceptualize a thought as if a physical object, you gain the power to exercise dominion over it...just like you would throw out an old pair of shoes, you can eject a unhealthy thought from your mind.

3. **Your brain can only process one dominant thought at a time.** In **Man's Search for Meaning (1959)**, Victor Frankl wrote about his time in a concentration camp. As horrible as his existence was, he was able to take his mind away to another place: visualizing himself teaching in front of a student body. That thought was dominant over the misery of his real world.

PAUSE…TAKE A BREAK…WE HAVE A LOT MORE TO COVER BUT PERHAPS IT'S TIME TO STRETCH OR RELAX.

OK, now let's delve into a little bitty of the nitty gritty of time management.

First and foremost I want to speak about clutter…. Yes, clutter. Clutter is the enemy of effectiveness.

CLUTTER IS THE ENEMY

This is how my garage used to look. It was totally cluttered. I could not find anything when I needed to. I had not yet learned the saying: *"A place for everything, and everything in its place."*

118

Then, one day, my wife had a suggestion. She told me that she would never cook another meal for me until I cleaned the garage. So, I did. Here's the point: **the act of discarding and organizing can be liberating.**

119

And you know what? My wife did me a favor. Simply by getting rid of all the junk, the clutter, my garage became much more functional. I had room to exercise and meditate. I could finally find items that I had stored there. I could hold my classes.

120

The garage example is a metaphor. We all have both physical and mental clutter in our lives. It may be in your garage, or on your desk, or in your mind—that sense of being overwhelmed by too much to do. Wherever, the act of discarding and organizing can be liberating.

121

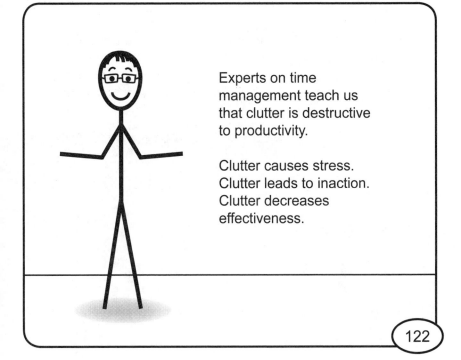

Experts on time management teach us that clutter is destructive to productivity.

Clutter causes stress. Clutter leads to inaction. Clutter decreases effectiveness.

122

"A dramatic reorganization of your home (or office or garage) causes corresponding dramatic changes in lifestyle and perspective. It is life transforming…when you put your house in order, you put your affairs and your past in order, too. As a result, you can see quite clearly what you need in life and what you don't, and what you should and shouldn't do."

The Life-Changing Magic of Tidying Up: The Japanese Art of Decluttering and Organizing,

Marie Kondo (Ten Speed Press, 2014)

123

As Ms. Kondo said in her very popular book, decluttering can be life changing...and not just in a physical sense. You see, most of us have brains like a vending machine. You put in a couple of items, and then something falls out.

Time management experts suggest that we develop habits and systems for helping our brains process, organize, and retain information.

> *"The short-term memory part of your mind—the part that tends to hold all of the incomplete, undecided, and unorganized "stuff"—functions like a RAM on a personal computer. As with the RAM, there's limited capacity; there's only so much 'stuff' you can store in there and still have that part of your brain function at a high level. Most people walk around with their RAM bursting at the seams. They're constantly distracted, their focus disturbed by their own internal mental overload."*

Getting Things Done, David Allen
(Penguin, 2001)

The quote above is from David Allen, one of the top thinkers in the U.S. on the subjects of time management and productivity.

Allen suggests that by developing strategies and techniques for collecting and storing information, one can achieve a "mind like water."

A MIND LIKE WATER

When Allen proposes that you want "a mind like water," he is suggesting a mind free of clutter. Think of a calm lake on a beautiful sunny day. No ripples. No waves. An easy serenity. By developing systems for processing and retaining information, you free your mind for important functions like analysis and creativity.

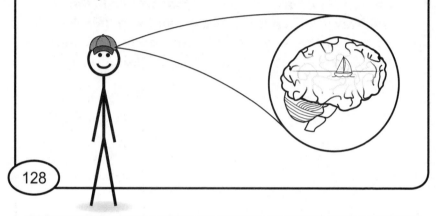

Here is my summary of the most important techniques for effective time management from David Allen's excellent book, *Getting Things Done—The Art of Stress-Free Productivity*:

1. Make your work area attractive and equip it with everything you need to work. You should enjoy spending time in your work area. Everything you want and need should be near at hand.

2. Create a filing system. Just the act of putting all material relevant to a particular subject in one place is a huge step toward better time management and organization.

3. Develop ONE list where you write or type EVERYTHING that requires your attention. By trying to remember too much, you clutter your brain. The point is to get it out of your mind and down on paper.

4. Move every item. As much as possible, every piece of paper, every e-mail, text or voice message should be acted on when you first see or hear it. Don't leave anything "for later."

5. Exercise one of three choices for every item. Make a decision to: (i) act on it immediately, (ii) toss or delete it, or (iii) incorporate it into your one list for further action.

6. Convert thoughts to action steps. Don't write on your list "consider this" or "analyze that." Put down specific action steps. Instead of "consider this," put down exactly what you will do (for example): "(i) read about ___, (ii) speak with Bill about ___, (iii) make decision about ___."

7. Once you decide on action steps, take action immediately if possible. Anything that you can do in two minutes, do it now.

8. Maintain a good "tickler" system. Any reliable method that reminds you what you need to do, and when, will help declutter your mind and improve your productivity.

9. Review weekly your systems for retention and productivity. Are your systems working as well as they should? Are you still burdened by trying to remember too much? Make changes as needed.

10. At least once a month, revisit your long-term goals. Are you making the right choices on a regular basis to move yourself closer to your goals? Or are you spinning your wheels? Make sure you are moving in the right direction!

By clearing the mind, good things happen. Here I am on a sailing vacation I took last month. Away from the meetings, the cell phone, the tablet and other daily stresses, I was quite productive. I wrote every morning, and I liked what I wrote.

Here I am after dinner last night. As you can see, I am trying to do too much at once. This is another form of clutter.

Sometimes you can accomplish more by trying to do less. Remember that thought as we will come back to it, but first I would like to bring up a new topic - PLANNING.

Planning simply means deciding **in advance** exactly what it is that you need to do in a given time period.

Many of us hate to plan. We live in such an action-packed society that we hurry around doing, doing, doing, and never step back to analyze what exactly is it that we are doing… AND WHY.

Perhaps you have heard the semi-humorous expression, READY, FIRE, AIM. That expression describes how many of us go about our days.

READY, FIRE, AIM

The problem with READY, FIRE, AIM of course is that energy is consumed "shooting" BEFORE the target is identified. That is **not** the right approach.

Instead, our objective should be to use our energy as effectively as possible by considering **in advance** where, when and how we wish to take action.

That means planning!

READY AND AIM
(PLANNING!)

ONLY THEN, DO YOU FIRE

You should spend at least ten minutes to plan each of your days. If you are a night person, do it the night before. If you are a morning person, do it the morning of.

Ask yourself questions like:

What is it that I want to accomplish today?

How much time do I have to do that?

Can I defer doing some items which are not important to another day?

Is there a logical order to doing what I need to get done?

By taking just ten minutes to reflect on what it is that you want to accomplish and how you are going to do so, you can dramatically improve the odds that **what you want to happen will, in fact, happen.**

As to planning your day, here's a new word you have probably not heard of ... just give me a second to type this.

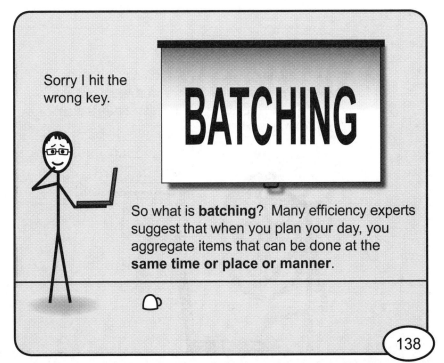

So what is **batching**? Many efficiency experts suggest that when you plan your day, you aggregate items that can be done at the **same time or place or manner**.

For example, let's say that you have to drive across town to accomplish X. You originally thought you'd do that around lunch time. But, when you started planning the day, you realized that later in the day you need to be across town to pick up Y. And, when you consider doing X and Y, you reflect on Z—a meeting you will be having across town in 2 days. You decide that X and Y can wait, and 2 days from now you take one trip across town to accomplish X, Y and Z.

You have **batched** these three chores into one trip— saving you lots of time.

The point of batching, which is a subset of planning, is to devise ways to bundle chores in a manner that allows you to accomplish each in less time than it would but for the bundling.

A close cousin of planning is preparation.

Thomas Edison said that "success is 90% perspiration and 10% inspiration."

I would like to suggest that "success is 75% perspiration, 15% preparation, and 10% inspiration."

141

The saying on the screen is my mantra for preparation.

By thinking ahead, by preparing, I believe that a person expends less energy in completing the task and, equally important, improves the chance of success.

PREPARATION
REDUCES
PERSPIRATION

142

"Give me six hours to chop down a tree and I will spend the first four sharpening the axe."

Abraham Lincoln

Sometimes I even prepare for important meetings or phone calls. I know that during these meetings or calls I will have a limited amount of time to influence those in the room or on the phone. I want to use my time as powerfully as I can so I decide—**in advance**—the key points I want to make in the meeting or call.

In doing so, I try to create for myself the most effective meeting or conversation possible.

Just a few days ago, I even prepared for a "chance" encounter.

I knew that I was going to be in an office suite where a man I had been trying to meet had an office. I had a rough sense of his schedule. My goal was to try to find a way to "bump into" him and ask for five minutes of his time.

And so I prepared by orchestrating how we might "bump" into each other. I prepared by thinking through what I would say to him when we did and, of course, how I would use our five minutes together if he was willing to give me some of his time.

As it happens, I got "lucky." My plan for meeting him worked, and he was gracious in giving me five minutes of his time.

Given how well prepared I was, I feel that I effectively presented my proposal to him. Time will tell what he'll do, but no matter what—with preparation—I moved the ball forward.

Important Person

As with most things in life, planning **taken to the extreme** can become a negative.

As Einstein said: "Nothing happens until something moves."

Some people overindulge in the planning process. They analyze and analyze and analyze because that can be easier than actually making a decision. Sometimes this process masks a fear to take action. At some point you need to take action, or at least make a decision that action is not the right course. Then move on.

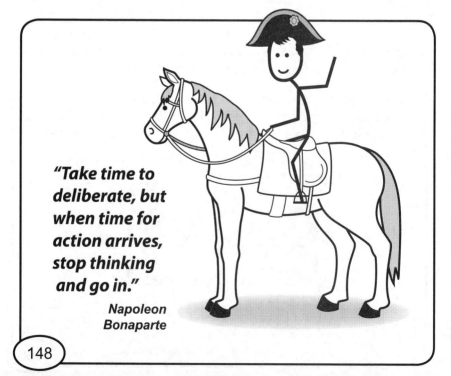

"Take time to deliberate, but when time for action arrives, stop thinking and go in."

Napoleon Bonaparte

"In any moment of decision, the best thing you can do is the right thing, the next best thing is the wrong thing, and the worst thing you can do is nothing."

Theodore Roosevelt

AND NOW ON TO A REALLY BIG TOPIC:

TO DO LISTS

The physical product which manifests all your planning and preparation is the To Do List.

I am pleading with you: PLEASE START MAKING TO DO LISTS!

Do you remember David Allen's point about "a mind like water"? He maintained that the calmer your mind, the more productive you would be. And he proposed that one way to develop a calm mind was to create systems for collecting and processing information.

That is the point of a To Do List. It is simply a system for using one place to collect and manage everything you need to remember on a going-forward basis.

There are many ways to create a To Do List. I happen to type my To Do List every morning as soon as I get up. Since much of my List from the prior day carries over, I am not crafting a new List every day. Rather I am revisiting the List from the day before and reworking it for the day ahead.

Many people use pen and paper to create a To Do List. Others use a cell phone notepad.

What counts is that you engage in a process of identifying what you need to do each day, and how and when you are going to do each task.

"Perhaps the most powerful time management tool is a daily list of activities that you create to serve as a blueprint for your day...Just as a pilot uses a checklist before every takeoff, effective executives take a few minutes to create a 'to do' list before they begin each day."

Time Management,
Brian Tracy *(AMACOM, 2013)*

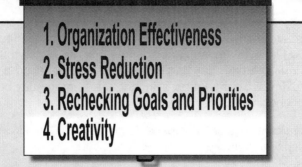

1. Organization Effectiveness
2. Stress Reduction
3. Rechecking Goals and Priorities
4. Creativity

There are many reasons To Do Lists work:

First, by forcing yourself to make a To Do List, you are organizing your time. You are thinking through all that you need to get done and writing it down. By thinking about what needs to be done and what doesn't, you create a framework for your day.

Second, a very important reason for making a To Do List is that by doing so you reduce stress. One cause of stress is the pressure you feel when you worry that there are things you're forgetting to do. When you organize your days, your stress may be reduced just by seeing your day visually—as opposed to grappling with all the pieces floating in your mind.

Third, making a To Do List requires you to rethink how you are spending your time and why. You will, of course, remember our discussion about goals and choices. Making a To Do List is a daily exercise in goal setting and choice making.

Fourth, making a To Do List can actually be fun. Think of it as writing a mini-novel with the main character being YOU. What you list is an act of creative planning—since the subject matter is YOU, your creative juices are heightened. You never know what thought or idea might arise out of the mere act of making a To Do List.

Speaking of To Do Lists, just when I thought I had seen every type of list or app or technique to help enhance one's productivity, I come across a low-tech system that is all the rage. It is called "bullet journaling", and it is chronicled in an edition of **Bloomberg News** (The Pen is Mightier, April, 2016).

To learn more go to **www.bulletjournal.com**.

It is described as the analog system for the digital age.

While you were contemplating the benefits of a daily To Do List, I was doing a little exercise... you know, using the downtime in my day.

158

Ouch...I think I hurt myself.

Oh well...time for a new concept...believe it or not, another word that begins with "P."

Want to take a guess?

159

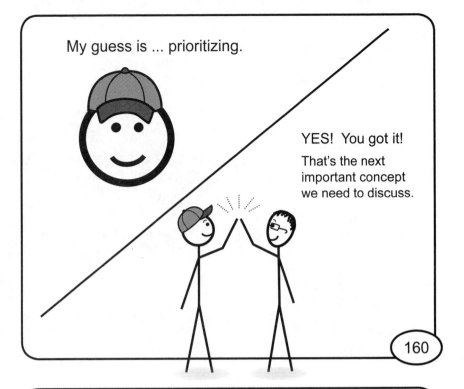

Most of us have too much to do and too little time in which to do what we need.

That is where prioritizing comes in.

Prioritizing is simply developing a sequence for what you do when.

A lot of well-known thinkers have addressed the subject of prioritizing. One of my favorites is Stephen Covey who wrote *The 7 Habits of Highly Effective People*.

Before we speak to Covey's views on prioritizing, however, let's address what I consider the most important takeaway from his book.

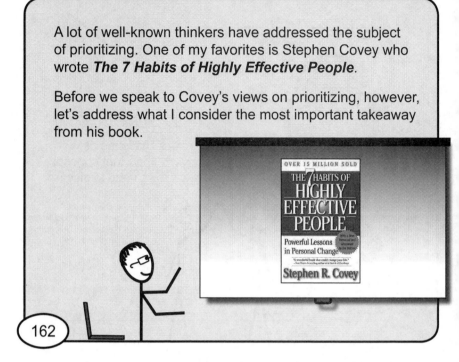

Covey teaches us that success is not an accident. Rather, success is the result of repeatedly doing those things that optimize the probability of a favorable outcome.

Successful people increase their odds of a desired outcome by developing positive regimens and habits...by creating behavioral patterns conducive to favorable results.

Let me give you a somewhat simple example.

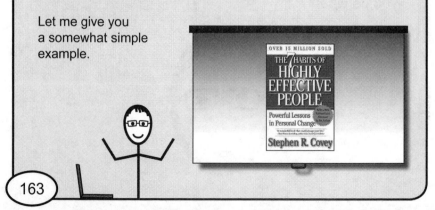

I used to always lose my car keys in my house. That was due to the fact I would put them down wherever I was when I emptied my pockets. But sometimes, the next day, I forgot where that was.

Then one day I decided that no matter where I was in my house when I emptied my pockets, I would **always** put my car keys on the dresser in my bedroom. Just that little act, that regimen in my day, has saved me tons of time and energy since I no longer waste time looking for my car keys.

164

Perhaps my car key example seems a bit pedestrian. But the overall point is not. When we develop routines in our lives, we do two things:

1. We cut down on wasted motion (like spending time looking for car keys), and

2. We preserve energy by reducing deliberation. As an example, I try to go to the gym at roughly the same time every weekday. By fixing into my schedule a definite time for exercise, I don't waste time debating with myself whether (and when) to exercise. Going to the gym is a regular part of my day...just like brushing my teeth.

165

Here is a riddle you might find entertaining.

"We are your constant companions, we are your greatest helpers or heaviest burdens.

We are completely at your command. Half of the things you do you might as well just turn over to us, and we will be able to do them quickly and correctly.

We are easily managed; but you must be firm with us.

Show us exactly how you want something done and after a few lessons we will do it automatically.

We are the servant of all great men and women—and of all failures as well.

We are not a machine, though we work with the precision of a machine.

You may run us for profit or for ruin—it makes no difference to us.

Train us, be firm with us and we will put the world at your feet. Be easy with us and we will destroy you.

WHAT ARE WE???"

HABITS

167

OK, now for Covey's views on prioritizing. Covey maintains that too many people prioritize by **reaction—doing what is pressing on them—** rather than by **proaction—doing what is important**.

Covey illustrates his point with a quadrant.

168

Covey recommends that when you are developing your To Do List, you put each task in one of these four quadrants:

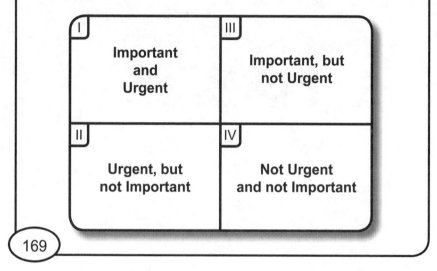

I Important and Urgent	**III** Important, but not Urgent
II Urgent, but not Important	**IV** Not Urgent and not Important

Then he suggests you prioritize.
And here is the question:

IN WHICH **SEQUENCE** WILL YOU PERFORM THE QUADRANTS?

Covey's point seems so obvious when you think about it...why clutter up your day doing stuff that may seem urgent **BUT UPON REFLECTION** is not really important to do?

The answer is:

First, of course, you do the items in Quadrant I—the important, urgent items.

What's next is interesting...Covey says that the next quadrant in sequence should be Quadrant III—the one containing tasks that are important **but not urgent**.

The next box to address is Quadrant II—the one containing the chores that are urgent but not important.

And finally, of course, Quadrant IV—which is neither urgent nor important.

RECAP

1. In developing To Do Lists, we need to always balance urgent items against important items, and select the important over the urgent whenever possible.

2. Effective time management means PROACTION (addressing the important) rather than REACTION (fending off the urgent). Many of us allow reactive forces to take over our lives - the press of e-mail and texts, the desire to engage with Facebook, Instagram or Reddit, the phone. We must try to replace reaction with proaction - the taking of affirmative steps to move us closer to our goals and objectives.

The difference in effectiveness between a proactive person and a reactive person is the difference between day ... and night.

There are many different ways to prioritize your "To Do" list.

Covey's suggestion of putting items in his quadrants does not work for me. I prefer Alan Lakein's suggestion of grading each item on your list A, B, or C. The A items are really important. Then B and C.

Sometimes I just highlight the important items. There is no one right way - the key is to prioritize.

"I cannot emphasize strongly enough: you must set priorities. Some people do as many items as possible on their lists. They get a high percentage of tasks done, but their effectiveness is low because the tasks they've done are mostly C-priority. Others like to start at the top of the list and go right down it, again with little regard to what's important. The best way is to take your list and label each item according as an A, B, or C priority...then polish off the list accordingly."

How to Get Control of Your Time and Your Life
Alan Lakein (Signet, 1973)

Another writer I enjoy, Brian Tracy, has written a book titled **Eat That Frog**. His book suggests that in sequencing, in deciding what it is that you do when, you always tackle your hardest project first.

"Mark Twain once said that if the first thing you have to do each morning is to eat a live frog, you can go through the day with the satisfaction of knowing that is probably the worst thing that is going to happen to you all day long.

(My) rule of frog eating is this: If you have to eat two frogs, eat the ugliest one first.

This is another way of saying that if you have two important tasks before you, start with the biggest, hardest, and most important task first. Discipline yourself to begin immediately, and then to persist until the task is complete before you go on to something else."

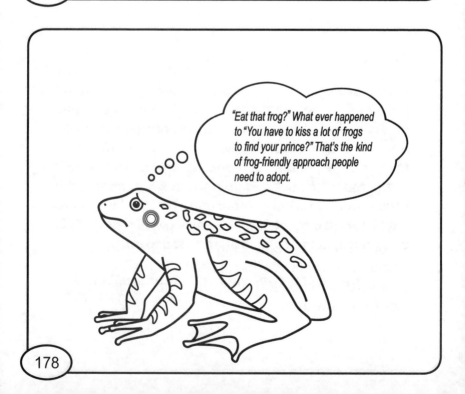

Of course I understand that running your day on the basis of your priorities is easier to say than do.

My point is just that you cannot let demands and desires run you. Make choices. Think about what you are doing and when. Sometimes urgent will overwhelm important and that is OK. My goal is to just get you thinking.

All this talk about To Do Lists may mask another important point: sometimes the effort to do too much (even if all items are important), is destructive to achievement.

STREAMLINING is about accomplishing more by doing less. An advocate of streamlining is Leo Babauta who believes that the best way to accomplish your goal is to do NOTHING BUT "to do" items that move you toward the goal.

"There's never been an age in which we are so overwhelmed with information and tasks, so overloaded with e-mails and things to read and watch, so stressed by the incredible demands of our lives.

I'm a firm believer in simplicity....Do less, not more, but achieve more because of the choices I make. Simplicity boils down to two steps: 1. Identify the essential.

2. Eliminate the rest.

I focus all of my energy and attention on that one challenge...I try to focus on one goal at a time... and not try to accomplish everything at once."

The Power of Less

Leo Babauta (Hyperion, 2009)

Leo Babauta has a point. Sometimes when we try to do too much, we accomplish less than we otherwise might.

• • •

"The hurrier I go, the more I fall behind."

Anonymous

Remember the picture of me trying to clear the table all at once? Well, ten seconds into my valiant attempt, I was on the floor cleaning up broken dishware and glasses. Took me 20 minutes. Had I instead cleared the table in two or three trips - instead of trying one - I might have spent an extra 30 seconds while saving myself 20 long minutes!

183

See the guy up on the screen. His name is Tim Ferriss, and he wrote an excellent book, *The 4-Hour Workweek*.

Ferriss makes a very important point about time management: that too many people equate A LOT to do with EFFECTIVENESS when, in fact, those are very different concepts.

184

"In the strictest sense you shouldn't be trying to do more in each day, trying to fill every second with a work fidget of some type. It took me a long time to figure this out. I used to be very fond of the results-by-volume approach.

The intent...is personal productivity."

The 4-Hour Workweek

Ferriss makes an important distinction between busy-ness and effectiveness.

Ferris suggests that those who are scrambling all day—from one activity to the other—may, in fact, be keeping busy at the expense of being productive. The goal is productive—the doing of those things that are going to move you closer to your goals.

There are times in our lives when we keep ourselves busy as a way to avoid introspection and hard choices. We tell ourselves that as soon as we "can" find the time, we will do whatever it is that is truly needed. Sometimes being busy is an excuse we create for ourselves.

BEING BUSY LEAVES NO TIME FOR SELF-REFLECTION

"For too many of us, the hustle and bustle of electronic activity is a sad expression of a life (without purpose). We feel busy...we are busy with busy-ness. Rather than figure out what to do with our spare minutes and hours, we pass our time with passing the time....We are always engaged with our thumbs, but rarely engaged with our thoughts."

Crazy Busy: A (Mercifully) Short Book about a (Really) Big Problem

Kevin DeYoung, 2013

One final point about busy-ness. It can often lead to overload. Our minds, like our stomachs, can sometimes get much too full. We need to lower the volume at times - to give ourselves time to recharge, to rejuvenate. The result is often a fresher mind and perspective - more effective, more creative, more receptive to new ideas.

"Unlike computers, human beings are not meant to operate continuously, at high speeds, and for long periods of time. Rather, we are designed to move rhythmically between spending and renewing our energy…We progressively burn down our energy reservoirs throughout the day. It's the equivalent of withdrawing funds from a bank account without ever making a deposit. At some point, you go bankrupt."

Building Renewal Into Your Workday
Tony Schwartz (2013)

OK, now on to a HUGELY important rule about time management and personal effectiveness.

THE 80-20 RULE.

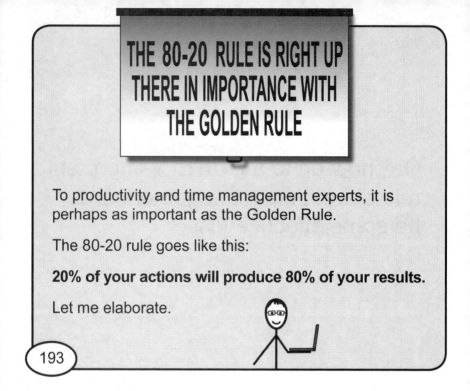

THE 80-20 RULE IS RIGHT UP THERE IN IMPORTANCE WITH THE GOLDEN RULE

To productivity and time management experts, it is perhaps as important as the Golden Rule.

The 80-20 rule goes like this:

20% of your actions will produce 80% of your results.

Let me elaborate.

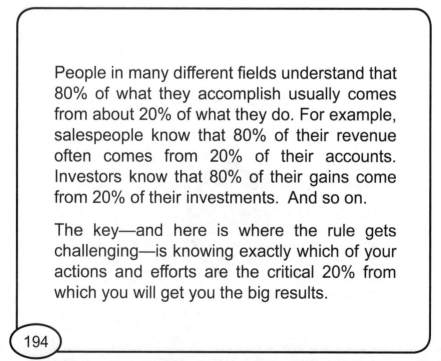

People in many different fields understand that 80% of what they accomplish usually comes from about 20% of what they do. For example, salespeople know that 80% of their revenue often comes from 20% of their accounts. Investors know that 80% of their gains come from 20% of their investments. And so on.

The key—and here is where the rule gets challenging—is knowing exactly which of your actions and efforts are the critical 20% from which you will get you the big results.

The 80-20 rule was first identified in 1906 by an economist named Pareto. One day, while tending to his garden, Pareto realized that 80% of his most vegetables were coming from only 20% of his plants. So he put more of his attention to caring for the high-producing plants, and the output from his garden increased greatly. No extra work: he just reduced the energy he was giving those plants that were not productive and reallocated it to the better plants.

That is why the 80-20 rule is so important. It does not require more work. Just smarter work.

People ask me how to incorporate the 80-20 rule into their lives. Here is how I respond:

Tell me one of your goals.

Tell me 5 things you are doing to achieve that goal.

Which of those 5 things is most likely to help you achieve that goal?

That's the thing to give the most energy and attention to.

In other words, if you are getting a lot of result ("80%") out of one or two activities ("20%"), those are what you should focus on. Please note that the actual percentage numbers are not relevant. What matters is the concept: Some activities pay back more than others; put most of your energies toward those that give you the "biggest bang for the buck."

OK, how about we take a little break?

**Close your eyes.
Rub your temples.
Take a deep breath.**

197

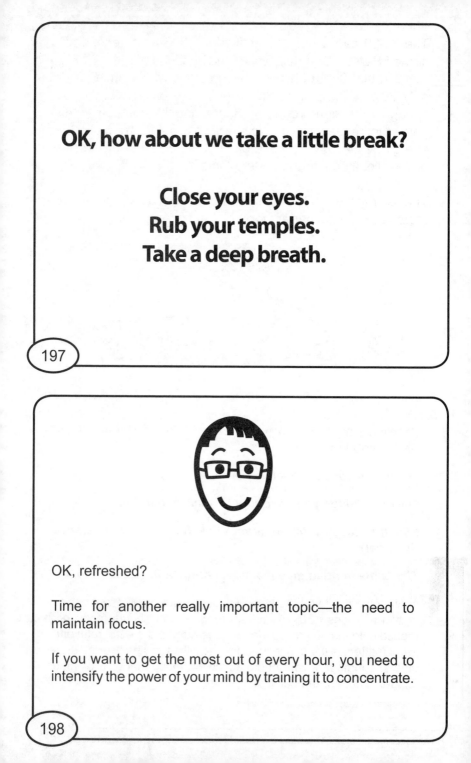

OK, refreshed?

Time for another really important topic—the need to maintain focus.

If you want to get the most out of every hour, you need to intensify the power of your mind by training it to concentrate.

198

OK, no harm…just a little smoke. Sorry about that, but in truth my little accident is not a bad segue to talking about focus. Over time, as you develop your ability to focus, you will find that you stop hearing noises like sirens and dogs barking. Your mind is so trained on one subject that you may miss sounds and events going on around you. That's generally OK so long as your house is not on fire.

If you want to get the benefits of powerful focus, you need to limit distractions—interruptions that take your mind away from what you are doing.

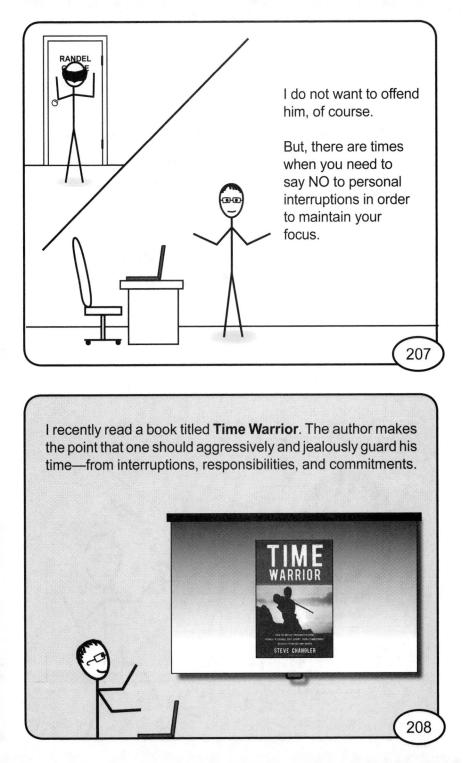

I do not want to offend him, of course.

But, there are times when you need to say NO to personal interruptions in order to maintain your focus.

I recently read a book titled **Time Warrior**. The author makes the point that one should aggressively and jealously guard his time—from interruptions, responsibilities, and commitments.

"And just how do you make time? It's made in your mind....With great swings and swipes of your samurai sword. You develop a brutal grace. Cutting out the unnecessary."

Time Warrior
Steve Chandler (MauriceBassett, 2011)

Chandler makes the point that sometimes you need to be warrior-like in guarding your time.

No harm done.

Let's move on before I cut something else off. Here's the key: if you want to work to your maximum potential, cut out distractions and discipline yourself to concentrate.

"Deep Work: professional activities performed in a state of distraction-free concentration that push your cognitive capabilities to their limit. These efforts create new value, improve your skill, and are hard to replicate....Deep work is necessary to wring every last drop of value out of your current intellectual capacity."

Deep Work: Rules for Focused Success in a Distracted World

Cal Newport (Grand Central Publishing, 2016)

"One reason so few of us achieve what we truly want is that we never direct our focus; we never concentrate our power."

Tony Robbins

213

AND, don't think you can focus when you are multi-tasking!

The fact is that when you try to do more than one thing at once, you dilute from the effectiveness of each thing that you are doing. In other words: 1 + 1 = 0.

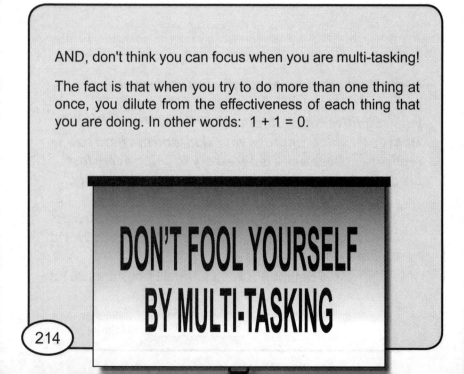

DON'T FOOL YOURSELF
BY MULTI-TASKING

214

Multi-taskers are supplanting focus with tumult. And that's a shame because when you really put all of your creative juices and personal energies onto one task—**and one task only**—the sky's the limit as to what you can accomplish.

Let me give you a few examples of what some people have accomplished—in incredibly short periods of time—when they put **all** of their energy to the challenge in front of them.

1. Pablo Picasso painted his most famous painting, *Guernica*, in less than two months. He was inspired to paint this great work after the bombing of his hometown (Guernica) in Spain during World War II.

2. Sylvester Stallone wrote the screenplay to *Rocky* in three days. Movie of the Year in 1977, *Rocky* spawned a whole series of *Rocky* movies and made Stallone an international star—changing his entire life in a flash.

"Now is the time to grab life by the throat and don't let go."

Sylvester Stallone

3. In 1987 the lead guitarist of the band, Guns N' Roses, Slash, spent three hours writing a song titled *Welcome to the Jungle.* This song became hugely popular and in 2009, VH1 named it the greatest hard rock song ever recorded.

4. In an amazing sports comeback, with 27 minutes left in the football game and trailing 35 to 3 in the 1993 NFL Playoffs, the Buffalo Bills rallied—scoring 38 points to win the game 41 to 38!

"While you can hold several chunks of information in mind at once, you can't perform more than one conscious process at a time with these chunks— without impacting performance....While it is physically possible sometimes to do several mental tasks at once, accuracy and performance drop off quickly.

When people do two cognitive tasks at once, their cognitive capacity can drop from that of a Harvard MBA to that of an eight-year-old. It's a phenomenon called dual-task interference....The lesson is clear: if accuracy is important, don't divide your attention."

Your Brain at Work

David Rock (Harper Collins, 2009)

Time is a gift. It is your opportunity to make something great happen. To illustrate your unique talents. To change your life.

Every day we get twenty-four 60-minute gifts to do something terrific.

Even one hour—let alone a day, a week or more—is a very powerful palette when it is the recipient of all of your attention.

"How did it get so late so soon? It's night before it's afternoon. December is here before it's June. My goodness how the time has flewn. How did it get so late so soon?"

Dr. Seuss

Wow! I can't believe it...we are coming to the end of our hour. I hope the time flew by for you as quickly as it flew by for me.

Just before we break, I want to list my favorite techniques and strategies for improving your effectiveness and time management.

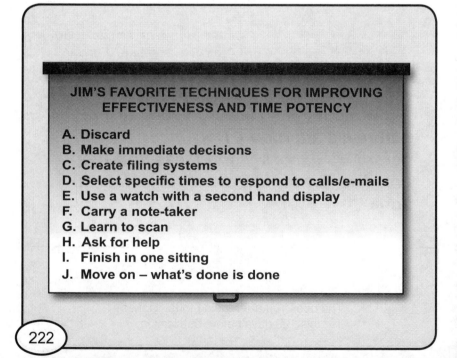

JIM'S FAVORITE TECHNIQUES FOR IMPROVING EFFECTIVENESS AND TIME POTENCY

A. Discard
B. Make immediate decisions
C. Create filing systems
D. Select specific times to respond to calls/e-mails
E. Use a watch with a second hand display
F. Carry a note-taker
G. Learn to scan
H. Ask for help
I. Finish in one sitting
J. Move on – what's done is done

A. Learn to discard quickly and without guilt. Pack rats hate this one. Learn to throw things away. To delete e-mails. More stuff means more junk and more clutter. The quicker you discard, the quicker you move on.

B. As to every item that comes into your day, make an immediate decision what to do with it. Whether a text, an e-mail, a voice message, a letter…whatever. Either: a) act on the item, b) discard it, or c) save it. Resist the impulse to "deal with it later."

C. Put every piece of paper, book or article that pertains to a single project in one place. For me, when I am starting to write a Skinny book I find that the act of putting all my research into one box helps me organize my thoughts.

The book you are reading today looked like this 120 days before publication.

D. Pick one or two times a day to answer voice messages, texts or e-mails. If you are working and allow yourself to be interrupted by continual pulls on your time, you will never get anything done well. Experts believe that when people are productively engaged, and then interrupted, it takes them 5-10 minutes to get back into productive thought after the interruption.

E. I recommend you wear a runner's watch with a digital second hand display. There is no better way I know of to keep you focused on the passage of time!

F. Keep handy some mechanism for taking down ideas that pop into your head during the day. By doing so you help reduce the stress caused by worrying that you will forget something you need to do.

G. Teach yourself to speed read. Like mental fortitude, speed reading is a skill that can be developed. Here is the single most important point to understand about speed reading:

YOU DO NOT NEED TO READ EVERY WORD OF WHATEVER IT IS YOU ARE READING (EXCEPT SKINNY BOOKS, OF COURSE).

You can usually get the intent of the writing by reading about 50% of the words.

For me, some combination of the following techniques gives me what I need to know:

(i) read just the first sentence of every paragraph,

(ii) read all words that are in bold, underlined or italicized,

(iii) read just the first and last paragraphs in a chapter,

(iv) scan vertically, not horizontally,

(v) read without mouthing any words (as best as you can), and

(vi) don't reread until you finish a page or several paragraphs, and only if you are convinced you missed something.

"The average reader can increase, by a minimum of three times, his present reading rate. (Speed) reading is a skill—a developed or acquired ability."

Triple Your Reading Speed

Wade Cutler, (Pocket Books, 4th Edition, 2002)

H. Never hesitate to ask for help. You can cut a lot of time out of any project by finding someone who has done it before and asking their guidance. No sense in reinventing the wheel.

Whatever you are doing, someone has most likely done it before. If you can find such a person and persuade him or her to guide you, you are going to save yourself a lot of time and heartache.

I. Whenever possible, finish a task in one sitting or segment of time. Parkinson's Law says that the time it takes to finish a project will expand into the amount of time one has to complete it. Do not let the amount of time you have control your progress. If you can finish a project in half the time you have to do so, you are ahead of the game.

J. Move on. The minute after you complete a test or a project stop thinking about it. Do not obsess over what you could have done differently, or better. People who worry about the past are wasting time because the die is cast, for better or worse.

Well, this concludes our session.

I hope you won't think of time management as a chore. Think of it as fun…like any challenge, something to be worked at but which can lead to great results once mastered!

The following pages summarize the ten most important concepts to remember about effective time management.

Thanks for stopping by. I enjoyed having you as my guest!

THE 10 MOST IMPORTANT POINTS TO REMEMBER ABOUT TIME MANAGEMENT

1. SELF-AWARENESS IS THE *SINE QUA NON*.

You can't go anywhere with time management until you are aware of how you are spending your time.

I recommend keeping a time journal for a week or so. Watch for areas where you might re-allocate your time expenditures.

2. GOAL-SETTING IS THE FIRST STEP.

There is no point to worrying about the passage of time unless and until you have identified those goals or objectives you are trying to achieve.

You are flying blind until you know the direction in which you should be traveling.

234

3. CHOICES ARE TOUGH.

Time management is ultimately about making choices.

You are gifted 24 hours every day. 168 hours every week. How you choose to use those hours is up to you.

Goal achievement is about making hard choices, about deciding among many competing demands on your time.

235

4. YOU CAN "CREATE" TIME.

Watch for ways to turn unproductive time into productive time. Look for gaps in your day or week when you can use time productively instead of sitting on your rump waiting for something to happen.

Increase your energy with exercise and healthy eating. The more energy you bring to an hour, the more powerful that hour becomes in moving you toward the realization of your goals.

236

5. PROCRASTINATION IS THE ENEMY.

Procrastination is so darn tempting. But, you must fight the impulse.

Try to think of yourself as either in forward or reverse. Either you are moving toward your goal which is good, or away from your goal. When you are standing still, your goal is most likely moving away from you.

237

6. AIM FOR "A MIND LIKE WATER."

If you can declutter your work area, your life and eventually your mind, you increase your effectiveness dramatically.

Clutter is an impediment to productive, powerful thought.

When you declutter your mind, you liberate it!

7. PLANNING AND PREPARATION ARE WORTH THE EFFORT.

By contemplating in advance what you want to accomplish with a particular event or in a specific time period, you increase the prospect that you will achieve what you set out to do.

8. WHEN YOU PRIORITIZE, YOU SEPARATE THE WHEAT FROM THE CHAFF.

Prioritizing means deciding what you are going to do when.

By organizing your day and life in terms of what matters most, you increase the probability that you will get to where you want to go.

One way to prioritize is to remember the 80/20 rule, which says that 20% of your activities will result in 80% of the progress toward your goals.

9. SINGLE-MINDED FOCUS IS WHERE IT'S AT.

By cutting down distractions and bringing lasered focus to the task at hand, you multiply the power of your effort exponentially.

Distractions are dream killers. They dilute your braininess. When you decide to work, then work, and do not let interruptions from third parties interfere with the effort.

10. PICK AND CHOOSE THE TIME MANAGEMENT TECHNIQUES THAT WORK FOR YOU.

We have identified time management techniques that increase efficiency. Some may make sense to you, others not.

Experiment and try different ideas. The key is to strive to use every hour you have as effectively as possible.

242

Time to go! Hope to see you again soon!

243

The
End!

CONCLUSION

We here at **The Skinny On**™ hope you enjoyed this book. We would love to hear your comments.

My personal e-mail is jrandel@randmediaco.com

Thanks for your attention, and may time always be on your side!

Warm regards,

Jim Randel

FURTHER READING

Here's a list of some of the books and e-books we read in preparing **The Skinny on Time Management**:

Banishing Multi-Tasking from Our Repetoire, Christian Jarrett (2013)

Break-Through Rapid Reading, Peter Kump (Prentice Hall, 1998)

Building Renewal Into Your Workday, Tony Schwartz (2013)

Crazy Busy: A (Mercifully) Short Book about a (Really) Big Problem, Kevin DeYoung (2013)

Creative Time Management, Jan Yager (Hannacroix, 1999)

Deep Work: Rules for Focused Success in a Distracted World, Cal Newport (Grand Central, 2016)

Eat That Frog!, Brian Tracy (Berrett-Koehler, 2007)

Future Shock, Alvin Toffler (Bantam, 1970)

Getting Things Done, David Allen (Viking, 2001)

How to Get Control of Your Time and Your Life, Alan Lakein (Signet, 1973)

How to Manage Time: Ultimate Tips for Effective Time Management, Neil Workman (Amazon Publishing, 2015)

Manage Your Day-to-Day, (Amazon Publishing, 2013)

Man's Search for Meaning, Victor Frankl (Beacon Press, 1959)

Mindful Tech: How to Bring Balance to our Digital Lives, David Levy (Yale University Press, 2016)

One Hundred Ways to Motivate Others, Richardson and Chandler (Career Press, 2012)

Remember Everything You Read, Stanley Frank (Avon, 1990)

Speed Reading for Professionals, Wechsler and Bell (Barrons, 2006)

Smarter, Faster, Better, Charles Duhigg (Random House, 2016)

The 4-Hour Workweek, Timothy Ferriss (Crown, 2007)

The 7 Habits of Highly Effective People, Stephen Covey (Simon & Schuster, 1989)

The 25 Best Time Management Tools & Techniques, Dodd and Sundheim (Peak Performance, 2005)

The Autobiography of Benjamin Franklin, Benjamin Franklin (1790)

The Life-Changing Magic of Tidying Up: The Japanese Art of Decluttering and Organizing, Marie Kondo (Ten Speed Press, 2014)

The One Minute Manager, Blanchard and Johnson (William Morrow, 1982)

The Productivity Report, Chris Bailey (Crown, 2016)

The Power of Focus, Canfield, Hansen, Hewitt (Health Communications, 2000)

The Power of Less, Leo Babauta (Hyperion, 2009)

The Time Trap, Mackenzie and Nickerson (AMACOM, 2009)

Thinking Fast and Slow, Daniel Kahneman (Farrar, Straus, 2013)

Time Management: How to Get 12 Hours Out of an 8 Hour Day, Natalie Johnson (Amazon Publishing, 2014)

Time Management: How to Get More Done in a Multi-Tasking World, Michael Reese (Amazon Publishing, 2014)

Time Management, Brian Tracy (AMACOM, 2013)

10 Minute Time Management: The Stress Free Guide to Getting Things Done, Ric Thompson (Amazon Publishing, 2014)

Time Power, Brian Tracy (AMACOM, 2007)

Time Warrior, Steve Chandler (Maurice Bassett, 2011

Triple Your Reading Speed, Wade Cutler (Pocket Books, 2002)

Work Less, Do More, Jan Yager (Sterling, 2008)